for Julia: "God Winds" p.59

VISIONS OF HOPE:
VOICES OF AMERICANA

BY

REV. DR. MARY B. JOHNSON

"Stand at the crossroads and look! Seek the ancient paths. Ask where the good way is and walk in it, and there you will find rest for your souls."
Jeremiah 6:16

DEDICATION

This book is dedicated to all of our ancestors and family members who have left a great legacy in Americana by demonstrating what it means to live simply, love greatly, and walk courageously. They have enriched every path they walked, always believing in the best of the American Dream, while continually manifesting a generous spirit and a loving heart in the face of adversity and pioneering challenges. While being teachers of patience and wisdom, they have also left a legacy of a passionate love of freedom, life, music, art, learning, nature, God, country, writing, people, and the land. Their vision of hope for better days and their faith in the American ideals of freedom, honesty, hard work, and independence still lives in the hearts of all they touched. For that reason, they will always remain greatly beloved and live on in the souls of all those they enriched, even as they remain in the memories shared in these poetic visions of precious times and places in the by-ways of Americana. May their spirits continue to fly free in our hearts! While acknowledging the contributions of all our American ancestors to the country each of us loves, this book is respectfully dedicated specifically to the beloved memories of:

Jon Erik Johnson (1964-2007)
Virginia Miller Boatman (1920-2000)
Samuel Arthur Boatman, Jr. (1917-1954)
Virginia Armstrong Johnson (1905-1998)
John Erik Johnson (1904-1971)
Samuel Arthur Boatman, Sr. (1893-1956)
Beatrice Turner Boatman (1897-1984)
Mary O'Dell Miller (1897-1948)
Harvey Henderson Miller (1890-1968)
Joseph Porter Turner (1856-1948)
Jemima Williams Turner (1858-1944)

Visions Of Hope: Voices Of Americana
By
Rev. Dr. Mary B. Johnson

Copyright © 2008 by Rev. Dr. Mary B. Johnson

All book rights reserved including the right of reproduction in whole or in part in any form.

No part of this book may be reproduced without the express written permission of the author who may be reached at the email address of: revdrmarybeej@gmail.com

PURCHASING: This book may be purchased online at the Create Space E store available at:
http://www.createspace.com/3338341 **or**
Amazon (www.amazon.com**). Directions as to how to purchase additional copies may also be available by contacting the author at the Email address above.**

Published in the United States Of America
First Edition
ISBN # 1434846423
EAN 13:# 9781434846426

Custom Books Publishing
Web Site: www.createspace.com

Acknowledgements:
"The Guardian" and "Wisdom Calls" have been previously published in "The Keene Sentinel".
A special thank you to Arnold E. Johnson for creating the original copyrighted photographs of Americana.
Old Family photos on page 5 are from Dr. Karl Boatman.
Graphic design has been created by using Print Shop, Microsoft Publisher, and Adobe Acrobat.
All graphic arts & book design are by Rev. Dr. Mary Johnson.

VISIONS OF HOPE: VOICES OF AMERICANA

Table Of Contents

Title Page	i
Dedication Page	iii
Acknowledgements	iv
Table Of Contents	v-vii
Prologue: **Americana**	1
Section I: Western Ways and Prairie Days	3
Forgotten Times	5
Horizons	6
Tales Of Old	7
Indian Eyes	8
The Family Farm	9
Light, Sweet, Crude	9
The Voice	10
A Tattered Family Blanket	11
The Old Corner Store	12
August	13
Mysteries	14
Colorado Reflections	14
Deadwood	15
South Dakota Skies	15
Prairie Winds	16
Sunflowers	17
Section II: Country Roads: Mountains, Hills, And New England By-Ways	19
Country Roads	21
Forever Young	22

VISIONS OF HOPE: VOICES OF AMERICANA

Table Of Contents

Title	Page
Perspective	23
Covered Bridges	24
Our Town	25
School Is Out	26
Old Roads	27
The Guardian	28
Sugaring Season	29
Autumn	30
September Rays	31
Mother	32
Falling Leaves	33
Farmers Market	34
Together	34
By The Wayside	35
Round About	36
Awareness	37
The Altar	38
The Sentinel	39
New England Flood	40
Planting Season	41
Section III: Rivers, Lakes, Oceans, And Bays	43
The Call	45
Water Views	46
Ocean Summers And Lighthouse Days	47
Brothers	47
Sister Of The Sea	48
The Ocean Rose	49
Waiting	50
Destiny	51
Cape Cod	52
Homeward Bound	53

VISIONS OF HOPE: VOICES OF AMERICANA

Table Of Contents

Title	Page
City Skies And Country Songs	**54**
Tides	**55**
Lighthouse	**56**
Section IV: Memories, Places, And Faces That Stay	**57**
God-Winds	**59**
Better Days	**60**
Sisters	**60**
Wedding Song	**61**
Love	**62**
Preparation	**63**
American Heroes	**64**
Wisdom Calls	**65**
Whispers Of Hope	**66**
The Path Not Taken	**67**
Wishes	**68**
Recovery	**69**
Remembering Days	**70**
Harvest Hellos	**71**
Epilogue:	
By-Ways	**73**

Prologue

BY-WAYS

By-ways beckon promising priceless
Unknown surprises around every turn
Clean of commercial strip malls greed
As we are on the road once again free
With smells of wood smoke wafting
Through magic golden falling leaves
Showering mysterious paths ahead
With treasured gifts blanketing the
Hum of soft engine sounds while
Warm friendly car heat wraps itself
Like a blanket against the Autumn
Chill as little ones nap securely in
Back leather seats curled up nodding
Dreams of new adventures emerging
Beyond crowded highways exploring
America's forgotten historic By-ways
As we are on the road free once again.
Mary Bee Johnson 11/4/07

SECTION I

WESTERN WAYS

AND PRAIRIE DAYS

FORGOTTEN TIMES

Old Oklahoma photos of wonder form
Covered Bridges in the Mind
To another place and space
Bringing transitions of magic mood
And newly found compositions of
Forgotten Times with memories of a cherished
Childhood rich with generous relatives
And fun loving cousins running free at
Enormous family gatherings with
Tales told of Days of Old while we feasted at
Scrumptious dinners looking forward to
Harvest Time making, stirring, and preserving
Mounds of sweet apple butter in big black iron
Bubbling kettles steaming outdoors with
Cinnamon rich aroma wafting temptingly
Under the pecan tree groves in the fields
Over glowing open wood fires while
Wise women of the family gathered
Lovingly around patting and chatting with
Each of the Little Ones sharing knowledge
Through all Time of how fortunate we
Are to be blessed with a faithful, wonderful
Extended family increasingly rare today.
Mary Bee Johnson & Carolyn Barber 6/29/07

HORIZONS

Distant viewpoints of long sought goals form
Horizons of Hope today reaching into what
Seems infinity transcending Time where
Pioneers from another Age wandered without
Boundaries across vast expanses of Prairie
Wilderness worn with wind howling songs of sad
Repose as travelers froze in sudden blizzards
Where vanishing horizons snow-bound still
Beckoned exhausted families to forge forth with
Faith that Freedom's light waited at the end of
The long trail where Healing Horizons offered
Gifts graciously filled with rest for weary souls
Promising security for struggling pilgrims who
Faithfully finished Life's journey with open eyes
Fixed on Horizons of Vision ignoring Winds of
Fear knowing that perseverance produces
Presents of Peace for those believing God cares.
  -Mary Bee Johnson 12/3/07

TALES OF OLD

The weather worn Old Man sat in the parlor corner dressed
With pride reflected in spit shined polished boots of the best
Leather as great grandchildren sat sleepy at his feet
Transported back in tumultuous times to meet:
"The Texas Turner Boys, gutsy bred who rode
As tornadoes with grit in the eyes, fearless and bold,
Daring and driven brothers quick on the draw
Herding cattle hard in hellish heat where the only real law
Was a man's word and sturdy pearl handled Colt forty-five
With the strength, skill and will to stay alive,"
Said Great-Grandpa Turner, warmly hugging
The little ones on his lap, bed time delaying
Some more while another gripping tale or two was told
Of awesome Oklahoma pioneer Days of Old
Vivid with Indian massacre stories replete with scalping
While he rode bold with the U.S. Cavalry scouting
Trails trying to capture fierce Geronimo before the sly
Warrior fox could stop Indian Territory from opening by
A hungry grand stand rush of settlers as wagons raced and
Prairie strong Sooner Pioneers claimed Oklahoma land
Where the family farm eternally stands in Yesterday-
While vivid memories replay of Tales of Old today
Told by Great-Grandpa JP Turner as he sits in the best corner
Parlor chair of my mind as a Beloved Guest of Honor.
    -Mary Bee Johnson 9/8/07

INDIAN EYES

Indian eyes stare searchingly above the old autograph
Scanning new horizons from the ancient photograph
Peering fearlessly above a white-woman's gown
Sheltering gnarled, work-worn, wisdom hands, brown
Skinned, skillfully cradling prairie babies still breast fed
While churning butter, nursing sick, burying the dead,
Tending stock, plowing land, evading locust swarms,
Surviving drought, fire, flood, and Western storms.

Ancient hands eternally open now revealing
Long hidden, shame formed, family secrets uncovering
Ancestor's old photos teasingly Time-Bound
Leading Homeward to windswept Sacred Burial Ground
Holding sun baked, half-breed fingers tearing time away
Touching white hands of a great grand-daughter today
Reverently seeking strength in a wisdom filled line,
Oh Indian Great-Grandmother of mine.

-Mary Bee Johnson 6/26/06

THE FAMILY FARM

The old farm stands forlorn now with skeleton sighs of happier days
As pink-cheeked little ones frolicked in harvest fields fascinated to see
Cheery chickens clucking while horses nuzzled close always
With soft snorts and sudden starts under the red rich apple tree
In dawn filled daring days when love blessed children ran free
Feasting on bountiful fresh food from Mother's garden all day
Still growing strong when rich milk streamed free for all to see
In the magic Open Barn glorious with new mown pasture hay
As mice scampered and kittens played greeting another new born day
Where Daddy stood with strong hands in rich black earth all around
Speaking of Sacred Soil to the little ones assembled again today
Silently understanding our connection to the Hallowed Ground
Beneath our bare feet as earth blew away blood red in the Dust Days
Driving Death Winds in shut doors surrounding Depression empty arms
Leaving supermarket food grown on poisoned land in Corporate Ways
While Empty Earth endlessly mourns for forsaken Family Farms.
Mary Bee Johnson 6/20/06

LIGHT, SWEET, CRUDE

Like magic apparitions black against Oklahoma skies
Oil derrick rigs rose strong defiantly demanding
Unquestioning worship from Depression starved men
Who labored long days and nights extracting
Liquid black gold crude from the depths
Of ancient Indian territory while the
Old Creek war chiefs gathered in Okmulgee
Town square in the hot evenings wondering
What new desecration the white men were bringing
To sacred hunting grounds now dead with red dust
Blowing into the cracks and crevices of shacks filled
With hungry people choking on dust storm dirt
Watching their fathers' Spirits slowly die
As men were forced to desecrate the holy earth
To buy bread to feed their starving families.
Mary Bee Johnson 2/4/08

THE VOICE

Sonorous, deep, resonating,
The Voice of Vision always remains
Soulful, seasoned, surrounding, removing
Fear with Father's voice cradling tears that still contains
Living comfort with Perfect Poetry cascading
Crowding, crashing, through Poverty Corners of Prairie Life
Bestowing Riches of Laughter, Love, and Learning
Amidst the Tornado Seasons of Struggling Strife
Filled Failed Farming followed by Flooding
Rivers destroying Home and Lands
While still starting over anew always persevering
He Built again, home made with strong carpenter hands -
While steady The Voice of Hope is still remaining
Strong in the fear filled anxious places
Of open childhood Hearts while Guiding
Now into fresh creative serene spaces
Father stays soothing, upholding, encouraging
Even while, yet young, on a November night he died
The Voice still remains strong with Poetry ringing
Clearly through time while the Sounds stay always inside
As The Voice of Truth and Love remains Eternally Living.

Mary Bee Johnson 11/8/06

A TATTERED FAMILY BLANKET

The worn patchwork quilt containing Daddy's shirt stitched
To Mom's apron remnants joining Grandpa's blanket pieces
Combined with family clothing unknown is wrapped closely
Now over cold laps under warm patchwork perfect
Protection stitched by Grandmother's loving hands
Resting now in God's tender care timelessly
Reaching out again to snuggle serenely around
The little ones resting securely today on Mother's chest
Watching snow falling like a white winter blanket
Beyond the wide world filled window pane
Where curious eyes survey the cold storm
Comforted with dreams of warmer days to come;
Nestled silently dreaming together of healing Spring hopes
Bringing new life beyond crystal winter graves covering
All living nature where long nights and shorter days
Reveal that Families are like patchwork quilts -
Individual Lives pieced closely together into one
Beautiful pattern radiant with memories eternally
Bound by love stitched into a strong protective covering
Intertwined with Golden Memory Threads
Bonding Spirit to Spirit throughout All Time
Transforming God's winter white blanket into dancing
Patchwork snowflakes releasing Resurrection's promise
Of New Life emerging from every dying seed -
Promising Flower Filled Fields of Spring Perfection
Revealing that Love is always stronger than Death.
Mary Bee Johnson 3/4/07

THE OLD CORNER STORE

Faithfully waiting where the cool breeze
Blows through shaded porches on hot days
Proudly stood the Old Corner Store,
A marvelous Magic Palace with
Penny candy and Grape Nehi soda pop,
Perfect cold nectar with crisp dill pickles
Delicious straight from the old crock
Where warm neighborhood dogs rested
From the heat, licking friendly hands
Grateful for little treats shared freely in hard times
When neighbor extended a helping hand
To all in need with no questions asked at
The Country Store where credit was good
And a man always stood on his word
Until progress passed us by at the Corner Store
For Walmart and credit card debt with
Collectors threats as mortgage foreclosures grow
While memories of the Old Corner Store
Offers a refuge for the struggling Soul.

Mary Bee Johnson 8/11/07

AUGUST

Kansas heat sits like hot gum stuck to warm
Windowpanes while stringy sticky humidity
Clings to clothing leaving sensations of
Wet washcloths wrapped in warm suffocating
Heavy sheets against skin dripping with
Alien August assurances that Summer
Takes a toll on the unprepared who forget
The price paid by dying Pioneer ancestors braving
August Prairie trails thirst crazed in covered wagons
Seeking Freedom from corrupted city ways
While modern suburban Sun worshippers
Emerge bikini burned with red skinned
Blistered faces and backs headed for cool
Swimming pools emitting chlorine vapors
While kids play screaming with energy as
An older crowd protects cold ice tea
Nurtured under sheltered sweaty poolside umbrellas
Dreaming of cooler days to come as
The Wise cower in air conditioned rooms humming
With hopes of Autumn breezes while remembering
Summer dug Santa Fe Trail pioneer graves
Still laying beside old Kansas highways
As the Wise hope for cooler September days to come.
Mary Bee Johnson 8/11/2007

MYSTERIES

Mysterious abandoned monuments proclaim the
Sudden disappearance of whole groups of ancient
Peoples in Colorado Mountains silently surrounded
By verdant canyons with sweeping views promising
New solutions to why old ghosts still walk protecting
Skeleton stones and broken bones of Indian adobes'
Sacred spaces in family rooms displaying complex
Civilizations in rock carved gorges advanced beyond
Our comprehension offering new perspectives on
Assumptions of the unending stability in our own country
Considering the thousands of years that precede us
Boasting grand achievements by unknown Americans
Now long gone softly whispering our names warning
Reminders that all Life is Sacred and fleeting in our
Vulnerable world where time stands still mourning
Mesa Verde Mysteries carved in Colorado canyons.
Mary Bee Johnson 8/23/07

COLORADO REFLECTIONS

Pristine waters under gird crystal glasses'
Reflections of Colorado mountain passes
Lovely lakes in high valleys of decision
Profuse with perfect creative precision
Framing wildflowers like jewels glowing
In fabulous fields of green grass offering
Emerald riches for the memories of those
Fortunate few who have viewed Flows
Of unending Beauty in Rocky Mountains'
Wind swept Sky rejoicing in Fountains
Of open vistas showing Eternity where
Bubbling creeks and carved canyons bear
Water reflecting mirrors of our dreams
With unending sparkling hopeful streams
Promising everything possible is unfurled
When we walk reverently in God's World.
Mary Bee Johnson 8/23/07

DEADWOOD

Deadwood town lays low today against the horizon framed
By golden rays of the setting sun illuminating sacred
Hunting grounds of South Dakota beautiful Black Hills
Still haunted with ghosts of Sioux Indian chiefs
Grieving silently over lost spaces pine tipped and
Raspberry filled fields shining with blazing wild flowers
Along bubbling cold crystal clear golden creeks
Jumping bountifully with trout where rocks glittering in the
Mountain sun once spread gold fever bringing greedy
Groping white men increasingly digging deeper scars in the
Wounded earth even filling pure clear streams with
Human waste while the thunder of guns violated
Centuries of silence as frightened deer herds fled
From green valleys seeking refuge in higher
Ground joining watching Indian eyes surprised at
Herds of White men joining Wild Bill and Calamity Jane as
Forests fell forming a bustling Gold town
Rich in graves, ghosts, dead men, and Dead Wood.
                          Mary Bee Johnson

SOUTH DAKOTA SKIES

Red rimmed sunsets glow golden on the prairie horizon
Where Badlands offer up gifts of dinosaur bones
To the enthralled children and adventurous
Travelers amazed at the beauty of South Dakota skies
Framing lush pine filled forests covering Black Hills gold
As Mount Rushmore looms presidentially reassuring
Visitors of the greatness of the American Dream
While Indian guides educate tourists from all nations
About the values of freedom and the American way
As dusk falls peacefully blanketing wildflower covered
Sacred Ground as time slowly heals wounds of yesterday.
                          Mary Bee Johnson

PRAIRIE WINDS

*Prairie Winds blow through my Soul calling
Me Home to where the buffalo stay
Free again amid the wildflower fields crowning
Flint Hills still star decked and Spirit kissed today
With morning diamond dew sparkling
On ancient, rich black unbroken earth
Protecting sanctified bones of my people crying
Out to me of forgotten Ancestor's eternal worth
With memories forged beneath blood of mine still seeking
To be Free where Spirit meets God's silver sky without walls
And ancient ghosts whisper old hopes with sighing
Symphonies calling me Homeward past Cottonwood Falls -
Etched with imprints of Prairie Schooners now following
Where Conestoga Wagons once streamed bravely along
Amidst the vast Vision promising Prairie eternally granting
Death defying Strength to those who hear its Sacred Song.*
Mary Bee Johnson 6/18/06

SUNFLOWERS

Sunflowers shine light into weary souls
After tornadoes roar overhead leaving silence
Scattering storm clouds opening skies of brightly glowing
Blue glass plates served with rich yellow colors on the
Palette of perfectly framed revelations of wheat fields
Preparing an incredible feast set just for you at
The bountiful places where Sunflowers bloom
Forever in sparkling Kansas fertile fields of old
Times where the trails still divide offering small town
Prairie memories wet with morning dew sparkling on
Childhood's irrepressible Joy that follows another
Sunshine day God has given to rapturously enjoy while
The love of friends and neighbors flows forth into waiting
Empty spaces filled with Hope for the hurting knowing that
The Lord still compassionately hears every prayer and brings
Beautiful plans for good to pass with restorative promises
Of abundant blessings and new beginnings in
Hard tumultuous times for those who persevere
As God restores the years that the locusts have eaten.
Mary Bee Johnson 1/31/08

SECTION II

COUNTRY ROADS:

*MOUNTAINS, HILLS,
AND NEW ENGLAND BY-WAYS*

COUNTRY ROADS

Country Roads unfold like ribbons in my mind
Taking me home to the West Virginia Hills where I was born
Where Grandma still welcomes us home at her open door
And Mother sings her sweet Appalachian tunes forevermore
While Grandpa shovels a little more coal into the B & O engine
Of a steaming train as his Railroad Conductor's cap proudly
Remains perched above blue eyes while I cling to his lap as we
Race once again through West Virginia mountains up steep turns
And over perilous canyons awesome with wonder displaying
Country roads like ribbons below on the lush green landscape
Winding our way through hills and valleys of freedom loving
Mountain folk with hidden stills in the ridges and rills
Where Lilies of the Valley still grow among wild strawberries
Sweet beside babbling brooks flowing by little white churches
Where old time gospel songs ring out from the rafters
As the puffing train engines whistle "Hello" to
Warm friendly people who still laugh at hard times
Knowing that Home always removes all tears
Wherever family remains standing strong
Supporting us in all our fears with ageless cheers
That ring out beyond time eternally leading us Home
On the by-ways of welcoming Country Roads.

Mary Bee Johnson 2/1/08

FOREVER YOUNG

Good-night West Virginia lullabies sung
Soft with Mother kisses accompanied by
Delighted snuggles of little sisters under
Feather comforters warming up bare feet
Chilled on wooden floors while the bedtime
Story was eagerly anticipated confirming
Fairies would fill the room as the moon rose
In hills magic with new thrills
And we whispered in the dark about all the
Important things while sharing secrets
Of where the Fairy Queen lived under the
Willow tree protected by the pond beside
Long weeping branches where we sat daily
Enjoying tea in acorn cups with frogs and
Mushrooms & sunshine magic companions
Of childhood while we held hands closely as
Only sisters can in comfortable invincibility
Aware that together we are forever young.

Mary Bee Johnson 11/15/ 2007

PERSPECTIVE

New Hampshire Hills hover in perfect precision
Granite Bound, rock ribbed, a richly clad decision
Melting Stone Hearts while the World Weary prays
For simpler days and smog clear sunshine rays
Still seeking hope filled healing in soft fresh air
Where eagles fly free above earth bound despair
As refugees flee smog filled city airways
For distant mountains promising new days
Sustaining seeking souls standing on mountain's lofty height
Seeing different perspectives now in dawn's new light
Of New Hampshire Hills offering Liberty's Call
Holding Sanctuary for the world-weary before they fall;
Fleeing urban upheaval spreading all around
As Weary Souls seek to stand free on shrinking Holy Ground.

Mary Bee Johnson 6/20/06

COVERED BRIDGES

*Like frozen fabrications
Of another Time crossing
Through many manifestations
Of Seasons sadly changing
Stand ancient bold bridges
Covered as monuments
Over streams and ridges
Showing old settlements
Living in simpler times
Leading Homeward to
Hospitality that rhymes
With cows that still "moo"
Warm wet welcomes for
Wandering lost strangers
Seeking healing in more
Safety and fewer dangers.*
Mary Bee Johnson 6/30/07

OUR TOWN

They say time passed us by in our town
In the hills where the water still flows
Free under our Covered Bridge
And the Post Office porch invites friends
And strangers to sit awhile and rest
In our country store rocking chairs
Shaded serene in the hot afternoon
Offering home-made ice cream, creamy cold
With friendly folks sharing a tale or two
Of busier days of old, but we like it this way
With no crime and a friendly "Hello"
Where we know our neighbors are fair
So we have no need to lock our doors or cars
Or go very far for what we need because
All the important things are already here
In Our Town where people still care.

Mary Bee Johnson 8/18/07

SCHOOL IS OUT!

Freedom flies on the wind rushing
Through fields of childhood filled
Memories of golden days richly offering
Lush long summers wandering thrilled
And unchained from demands stifling
With restrictions of adult confinement in
Narrow prison spaces of unthinking
Obedience to authorities dead within
Old text books silencing imagination now
Bursting forth in Summer's vacationing
Creative release to live free any how
We can beneath open skies where children see
Dreams forming visions where we may stand
On what we can possibly become and be
In God's rich plan for all His sons and
Daughters giving unlimited prosperity
Beyond earth bound limitations
And adult misperceptions.

Mary Bee Johnson 6/14/07

OLD ROADS

Old dirt roads slowly unwind
Opening views from another time
In bountiful beautiful by-ways
And free winding highways
Adorning New England hills
And vales where beauty fills
Jaded eyes of weary travelers
Seeking long lasting anchors
In shifting lonely landscapes
Rich with rare Pilgrim estates
Eternally announcing religious
Freedom while white gracious
Open churches proudly proclaim
God's hope that will sustain
A lasting Peace that still unfolds
At the final end of Old Roads.

Mary Bee Johnson 6/29/07

THE GUARDIAN

*Just an Old Woman, you may
Say, standing alone admiring
Flowers entranced with beauty today
Preserving ancient ways of soothing
Slower days appreciating every
Glimmer of flickering light she
Sees on displayed works of cheery
Handcrafted quilted Art in the
Farmer's Market where the Old
Woman stands prophetically as
Our Sacred Guardian of a bold
Forgotten Age where Worth was
Measured with clear Quality and
Not the enormous Quantities of
Corporate money buying our land
Void of any real respect or love
While Stripping our starving Souls
Quickly now destroying our Nation
With Strip Malls of empty holes
Greedy for consumer adulation.*
Mary Bee Johnson 6/9/07

SUGARING SEASON

Spring grows quietly invisibly
Beneath cold snow filled fields
Forming frost heaves over future flower buds
Beneath mud filled New Hampshire meadows
Hard with hidden frozen chilled memories
Of better times when playful birds flew
Singing in flowing Spring perfumed air
Now chilled with ice on the birdbath
While shivering cardinals consider strange
Sap Buckets hanging on leafless maple trees
Promising sweet flowing emerging nectar
From condensed earth's purifying flow
Journeying upwards through maple roots
Earth anchored in dying life metamorphosing
Miraculously into God's free flowing liquid gold
Tapped through wounded bark then carefully
Poured into boiling wood fired iron kettles
Steaming in ancient family sugar shacks
Condensing life essence of pain filled winter
Survival into Nature's Spring Gift soothing
Old Winter wounds with healing Maple Syrup.
Mary Bee .Johnson 4/28/07

AUTUMN

Autumn breezes blow gently with silver and gold
Threads of magic memories weaving transcendent
Glory shared in rich harvest seasons of life where
Pumpkins stand proudly in front of the Grocery Store
And Canning jars are eternally filled with bountiful
Wonders of Mother's garden abounding with provisions
Of resplendent riches from New Hampshire earth as sparkling
Glass jars stand proudly against the kitchen counter
As Mother labors long making more apple butter
For grandsons with big appreciative eyes admiring
Just the right manner she slowly fills the open Ball jars
With sweet cinnamon apple nectar from the apple orchard
Sharing ancient knowledge from days of old
Stooping low as the magic of Autumn in New England
Shines once again through red and yellow glowing
Maple trees resplendent with scarlet cardinals and
Perky chickadees cheeping a thankful chorus of song
For seeds abundantly shared from Mother's trembling
Hand as hummingbirds dance around the bird stand while
We glory together in the sweetness of another autumn day.
Mary Bee Johnson 2/2/08

September Rays

Late September summer days
Sit gently with glowing golden rays
Shimmering on yellow butterflies
Dancing in daring grace over blue skies
Blessing colorful fields of open flowers
Dew kissed with morning showers
While orange pumpkins ripen with glory
Under growing green mantles of vines
Winding silently through harvest lines
Of pilgrim tourists exploring the by-ways
And New England winding highways
Leading lovingly homewards always
To places of peaceful recollection
Inspiring a very careful selection
Of just the right gift from the land
Glowing at the Vermont roadside harvest stand
Welcoming Autumn as our Spirits reviewed
September days hoping old life will be renewed.
Mary Bee Johnson 9/3/07

MOTHER

Beautiful warm hands touch mine
Securely holding tiny fingers
Trustingly wrapped in hers,
While we walked slowly to the corner store
Anticipating just the right sweet treats
For warm Oklahoma Summer days.

Protecting me with a kind reminder
Not to talk to any old stranger,
We proceeded on our way with anticipation -
Welcoming sky reflected rainbows with little skips of joy,
Delighting in thoughts of peppermint sticks and cold ice cream,
Preparing for unending possibilities of adventurous forays.

Beautiful cold hands touch mine
Securely holding fragile worn fingers
Trustingly wrapped now in hers,
While we talk slowly of the old days some more
Anticipating just the right sweet treats
For New Hampshire evenings where the cool breeze stays.

Protecting Mother now with warm blankets and a reminder
Not to forget to take her medicines to escape danger,
We proceed with our lingering conversation -
Watching crystal reflected rainbows dance on the wall with joy,
Delighting in thoughts of good times and homemade ice cream,
As Angels gather preparing her for eternal adventurous days.

Mary Bee Johnson 8/1/06

FALLING LEAVES

Leaves fall slowly like yellow feathers gently drifting
Dancing earthward with delicate circling weavings around
Branches of the beautiful expansive golden maple tree
Outside open windows while smells of wood smoke
Caresses October cool breezes releasing revelations of cold
November winds coming soon when the perfectly dressed
Maple tree will stand stripped naked and barren with
Skeleton limbs anchored in snow covered ground exposed
Yet secure in friendly Earth knowing it will support
Vulnerable tree flesh sustaining an old friendship with the
Protection only a long relationship of Love can offer in hard
Cold Winters when icy blizzards bring killing winds in Life;
Yet the maple tree stands secure in certain wisdom that
Love is stronger than Death knowing that Spring always
Follows Winter's frozen grasp of stillness with green new
Leaves that will appear in due season for those who have
Enough Vision to believe that "Faith is the substance of
Things hoped for; the Evidence of things not seen."
Mary Bee Johnson 10/28/07

FARMER'S MARKET

Rich earth, God touched sacred
Creator of mother womb Life
Bringing a love affair to every
Farmer's soul who sees the Holy
In the mud; making decomposed
Essence of Life transform dying
Seeds into abundant glorious red
Strawberries and glowing green
Lettuce sparkling with morning dew
At the Farmer's Market where faithful
New Priests of the Earth offer another
Generation's creations of Love to all those who
Come to freely feast from the Temple of
Mother Earth's abundant healing gifts
Where God's Treasures are freely shared
With all Pilgrims at the Farmers Market.
Mary Bee Johnson 8/8/07

TOGETHER

On the heavens in each bright shining star,
On the earth in tender budding flowers,
In the morning sunrise shining afar,
In the cool refreshing Spring time showers,
In the freshly plowed fertile fields,
In the memories of all the passing years,
In the rich autumn harvest yields,
In all the life giving laughter and loving tears,
The ones we Love will always live on forever -
Etched in richly eternal golden shared memories
Surrounded by God's loving Grace that will never
Allow death to separate the shared love of families.
Mary Bee Johnson 6/8/07

BY THE WAYSIDE

The little white church by the wayside
Stands silent, worn, and quite forlorn now
Not many people go there anymore,
Although I remember long ago
When loving neighbors filled the pews
With prayers for all those in need and songs
Rang thankfully through the green Holy fields
With joy that God answered every prayer
In all situations and afflictions of life, death,
Suffering, birth, and marriage when we lived
Harmoniously with Heaven's plans, but that
Was long ago when Mom and Dad and I went
With Gram and Grandpa to the little Church
By the Wayside where lasting help was given
To all for free by many Pastors there with
Wisdom, but we've been too busy for years to
Go to church anymore with the divorce and
The kids on drugs, and it doesn't matter much
Anyhow, because they say tomorrow finally
The church doors will close forevermore.
Mary Bee Johnson 8/2/07

ROUND ABOUT

Round and round and around we go
Where it will stop we just don't know;
Progress, clarity, and traffic control
Necessitate a much bigger street hole
In the highways and by-ways
Of an America we no longer know
With detours around downtown below
Promising safer protected pedestrian flow,
Eventually anyway, our leaders assure us
While slowly we go bankrupt with no fuss
As vital access is blocked by construction's
Eternal promises to deliver manifestations
Of perfect population control Traffic Circles
While the rest laugh so very hard it tickles
Us into crying at wasted energy and time
For solutions that leave questions like slime
As round and round and around we go
Where it will stop we just don't know.

Mary Bee Johnson 8/3/07

AWARENESS

From another time the clip clop
Of horses hoofs on the concrete highway
Shocks the passer-by to recognize Life
Still exists beyond the cement prisons
Forming the highways and by-ways
Of a nation grown gasoline greedy going
Faster still in greenhouse choked smog
While our young see no stars
In smog covered skies with sighs
Wondering what could have been;
Until suddenly Awareness dawns that
The old fashioned Amish horse and carriage
Certainly works wonderfully better
Than all the death filled cars
Polluting skies and lives
And poisoning our broken land.

Mary Bee Johnson 7/6/07

THE ALTAR

Stone Walls meander through New Hampshire forests today
Moss covered, memory bound, spring wildflower decked, silent
Mysterious growth in sheep grazed pastures forgotten yesterday
When brave farmers fighting to preserve Union southward went
While weeping women prayed over our Underground Railway
Helping frightened slaves flee northward - Freedom Bent -
As farms stood unattended with farmer-soldiers far away
For few returned to New Hampshire fields, blood spent,
Rock bound, ghost haunted, forest covered, silent and unseen;
Where sighs too deep for words drift thru the green hills now
When sounds of "Taps" rings out once again on the green
Town Commons as shy Spirits touch the living who bow
To honor the heroic dead gathered round each Civil War statue
Memorializing supreme sacrifices of those who bled and died
Losing precious farms where forests grow today for me and you
Over sacred Stone Walls of timeless Altars for Freedom's Tide.

Mary Bee Johnson 6/19/06

THE SENTINEL

Misty mountain, changing moods
Reflecting heights that soar protecting
Surrounding New Hampshire towns
Basking in golden glorious colors of
Seasonal splendor while the mountain
Stands alone as a silent Sentinel since
Time immemorial solid like an old
Friend smiling a welcome to weary
Travelers homeward bound grateful to
See Mt. Monadnock still emerging as a
Granite monument God carved earth
Bound soaring heavenward reminding
Us that strength lies in endurance
Against the encroaching storms that
Threaten extermination of values we
Hold dear while angels dance atop our
Mountain guardian guiding us home.

Mary Bee Johnson 9/30/07

New England Flood

Streams of Sorrow
Seek dark Autumn's waters falling, creeks growing;
Flowing Cold River raging, flooding
Dams bursting below,
Suffocating Destruction flowing.

Cold Streams follow
Ice choked, Christ evoked praying, fleeing, grieving;
Winter wrapped weeping, freezing
Rivulets of Loss, haunted and hollow
Rivers of Despair endlessly streaming.

Springtime Streams grow
Earth enriched trickling, hoping, healing, singing;
Helping Wise Waters pouring, weaving
God's Gardens of Tomorrow,
Surrounding Bountiful Streams of Blessing.

Mary Bee Johnson 5/20/06

PLANTING SEASON

Teams of plow horses five abreast
Create a perfect picture of wisdom
Against the backdrop of lush green
Springtime Pennsylvania fields while
The Amish farmer patiently plows as of old,
In the same manner for hundreds of years
Shunning fancy ways and things that
Do not endure so that we may understand
That the Lord will also bless our simple labors
Of honest integrity in the vast Harvest fields of Life
As we plant Faith in fertile ground
Burying despair and overcoming strife while
Planting kindness in weed choked busy days freeing
A Harvest of Love growing with soft sighs
In rain drenched Stormy Seasons
Knowing that the old seed sacrificially
Dissolves and dies before promised New Life
Can emerge spreading growth patiently reproducing
While silently spreading Hope abundantly
In the Lord's planting grounds joining
Both Heaven and earth together rejoicing
As God's Kingdom continually is growing.
Mary Bee Johnson 6/10/07

SECTION III

RIVERS, LAKES,

OCEANS AND BAYS

THE CALL

Sea Born Breezes Beckon Me To Return
To where rivers seaward rush to their final turn
Homeward Once Again Spirit Winds are calling,
Bearing Sounds Of Sea Gulls Sighing
Over sluggish creeks' frosted chills
Past Problem Filled Haunted Hills
Holding Yesterday's rose rimmed dreams
While a rock ribbed Ocean Lighthouse still beams
Over tide filled bays where Harbor Bells toll
With memories sacred to my soul
Of God bound Kingdom Days
Decked in Ocean free ways
While a shimmering star crowned night sky still sings
Where we walked beneath Angel's Wings
Offering Healing To You And I Once More,
Along The Sky Blue, Spirit Kissed Sandy Shore.

Mary Bee Johnson 5/20/06

WATER VIEWS

Water forms a sacred substance
Mysterious beyond comprehension bringing
Life Forces to all earth bound
Creation where God sits enthroned in
Healing Streams of a perfect paradise
Reflected like glass in Carolina
Pools of sweet stillness where swim magic
Creatures of sacred form leading us
To a deeper awareness of the awesome
Preciousness of all that exists even while
Often assuming invincibility, forgetting
That Prairie rain comes and returns to its Maker
With western rivers roaring forth cleansing
Smog from California skies to Colorado mountain tops joining
Transformations of New Hampshire oceans joining
Cape Cod sea air evaporating heavenward once again to
God's heavenly home creating Kansas rain anew returning to
Earth again as life giving Missouri River water flowing
Seaward evermore abundantly revealing
God's eternal faithfulness in drought and pain.
Mary Bee Johnson 8/15/07

OCEAN SUMMERS AND LIGHTHOUSE DAYS

Rosebud Lips, Pink Fat Cheeks, A Girl Child Gift Quite Fine
With Tiny Fingers That Cling To Mine,
Like A Radiant Rose Bud Tenderly Unfolding,
Carefully Your Soft Small Hand I Was Holding
Watching In Amazement The Glory Of Seaside Ways
In The House Of Summer Days -
Not Far From The Ocean Waves Where You Pranced
With Seagulls Flying Free As Spirit Danced
Where Seashells Shine And Shimmering Seaweed Lays
In Ocean Summers And Lighthouse Days;
While I Remembered The Day You Were Born
As You Shaped Sand Castles On the Shores Of Time Reborn
Sharing Ocean Memories Once More
Holding Your Own Child's Hand Along The Sunset Shore
Where Ocean Roses Bloom Always
In The Memories Of Ocean Summers And Lighthouse Days.
Mary Bee Johnson 6/20/06

BROTHERS

Standing strong against the tide rushing unified
To bravely join in battle against the roaring waves
Brothers are scampering ecstatically with soaring sea gulls
Holding little fingers open to catch the wind
Laughing with utter joy in another Ocean Day
Running forever free over all the shores of yesterday
Still rich with emerald seaweed and sand castles
On beaches alive with little cousins and cotton candy clouds
Replete with shouts and childhood giggles discovering
Wondrous starfish, crabs, and seashell treasures
Brothers still remain forever joined holding hands always
In memories of ocean sunsets and seaside days while
Spirit treasures timeless thoughts of precious sons
Entrusted to a Mother's heart for a season and time.
Mary Bee Johnson 2/7/08

SISTER OF THE SEA

Silhouetted against time
Firmly framing evening sunset skies
Contemplating ocean autumn days
And mysterious ways of seasons reborn
Upon a sea kissed sandy shore
Sat my Sister of the Sun.

Serene against a changing landscape
Perfectly poised amidst the rising waters
Meditating on changing times
And fleeting days of time forlorn
Upon a rocky bound barren bay
Stood my Sister of the Wind.

Strong against the storm
Rising tall amidst the windy October sky
Rebuking fear filled possibilities
And covering dangerous wounds with healing hands
Upon exposed rain drenched raw earth
Lay my Sister of the Sea.

Mary Bee Johnson 10/14/06

THE OCEAN ROSE

Ocean roses stand as sentinels
Guarding shifting sands and
Weary souls from encroachers
Who would deny God's perfect
Act of creation offering eternally
Shared memories of sweet rose
Perfume drifting across wondrous
Waves while we stand amazed
At how sacred a flower can be with
Cascading tides crashing on timeless
Maine shores where only yesterday
We stood together transformed
By the life giving splendor of
One lonely ocean rose protected
Forever among thorns offering
Healing refuge to torn souls
Seeking safety from despair.

Mary Bee Johnson 6/20/2007

WAITING

I sit now in Portsmouth Harbor;
Ocean worthy but unused below
Deck except for tourists who forever
Stare at this ancient Gundalo
While they say this Old Boat
Has seen much better days
But you can't deny, I'm still afloat
Filled with Ancient Ways
When soaring sail power
Filled the rivers and bays and seas
Courageously sailing however
And whenever we please -
Remaining not guilty of pollution,
This creaky tied up Old Barge
Still stands proud with anticipation
That one day open hearts will be large
Enough to hear the Ocean Pray
Waiting for a deeper appreciation
Across time of a Simpler Day
Of respect for all God's Creation.

Mary Bee Johnson 6/19/07

DESTINY

Waves Crash Upon Broken Rocks In Motion
Rolling, Crackling, Pebbles Thundering
Into Ocean Shaped Pearls Of Perfection
Refilling Empty Storm Gouged Growing
Vacant Spaces Filled Anew Today
With Sacred Water Flowing Freely
Still Salty With New Life That Will Stay
While Wind Tossed Hungry Sea Gulls Wait Patiently
For The Right Rhythms Of Timeless Tides Changing
Seasons Revealing Truth That Has Been Concealed
Knowing That With Exactly The Right Timing
Destiny Will Provide Sustenance Now Revealed
In A Perfected Form That Is Far More
Abundant After Paying A Vigilant Cost;
For God Eternally Seeks To Restore
What Otherwise Would Certainly Have Simply Been Lost.

Mary Bee Johnson 10/15/06

CAPE COD

Cape Cod remains entrenched
Enriching Massachusetts Bays with sand
Shared with land eternally reaching
Out to welcome home pilgrims once again
Today who stand amazed viewing Plymouth Rock
From a water surrounded tourist perspective
Learning that Liberty belongs to the brave
Willing to stand strong in adversity
In all seasons of fear knowing that
Perseverance releases providential blessings
Beyond centuries of struggle
Where the land meets the sand
And roaring rivers flow freely to the sea
Releasing the spirit of Americana
Still extending open arms to refugees
From oppression and religious persecution
While Old Cape Cod reaches out anew today
With fingers of Hope to city dwellers seeking
Restoration and re-creation in cool breezes
And ocean tides offering release
From stress filled days and city ways.

Mary Bee Johnson 2/3/08

HOMEWARD BOUND

May your Spirit soar Free in these troubled days
With favorable forward winds pushing ahead
Guiding towards your unique Destiny always
Where the Journey of Life reveals instead
Of despair, a growing certainty that you already
Have all that is needed to accomplish important dreams
As long as the Course is held true and steady
Given to you, no matter what the lying storm screams -
God will be your faithful guide in fog and dark times
As you reach out anew with Hope and Love,
A Divine Light of Direction will beam that shines
Eternally below guiding homeward from above.

Mary Bee Johnson 6/7/18

CITY SKIES AND COUNTRY SONGS

City skies, lonely country sighs
Yet it seems you are there with old ties
In familiar restaurants and Boston Back Bay breezes
In multitudes of memories that seizes
My heart in shared familiar places
With sea air touched tunes that graces
Guitar chords in cool gardens carrying old time
Winds and country songs that rhyme
Whispering your sweet familiar name
Repeating that you are not gone, my son, but came
Clearly to be present everywhere now
For even when looking away your face somehow
Is smiling in cumbersome city corners hustling
With street singing musicians busy bustling
In ancient adored North End promising places
That you loved shining anew now in the faces
Of Cambridge street vendors selling fantastic flowers
Where again your broad smile showers
My memory with wonderful times we shared
Knowing now your Spirit can never be buried
By grief but lives on always in bustling city skies
And quiet Homestead country road ties
Where your beautiful Soul flies forever free
Of pains of earthly chains blessing us now eternally.
Mary Bee Johnson 7/23/07

TIDES

Spring sun shines on ocean tides as they unfold
Bringing Wind Songs to my heart
With rolling remembrances of days of old
Rhythms of Life when we were not far apart;
Although today suddenly seems to find
Shadowy silent tender thoughts floating
Freely of You ever present on my mind
With treasured timeless moments bringing
Your presence like the Tides closer today
Than the crystal cold blue roaring ocean wave
Rolling over my bare feet rushing to say
How many meaningful memories you gave
Graciously over all the passing promising years
Still living today silently and gently wiping away
Always with caring simplicity so many tears
By joyful shared laughter that will eternally stay.

Mary Bee Johnson 6/20/07

LIGHTHOUSE

Stormy seas scream that all is lost in seasons
Of despair when the weary traveler falls
Exhausted at the end of a long journey through
Hard days drowning in mysterious ways
Of desperate times until beginning to sink for the last time
No longer able to hold on to the life raft in the dark
Of a shouting storm demanding surrender
Of all we hold dear until mysteriously
In the darkest night of the soul of the doomed,
A divine Light shines with welcoming bells
Showing the way home to a refuge that is closer
Than we could imagine where a Lighthouse stands
Serenely on a solid rock amidst the sinking sand
And crashing waves granting a place of rest
For all the weary and lost sheltered now at last
Beneath the comforting arms of a loving God
Eternally offering refuge for all souls lost in any storm.

Mary Bee Johnson 2/16/08

SECTION IV

PLACES, FACES, AND

MEMORIES THAT STAY

GOD-WINDS

Friendship Is A Bountiful Breeze
Blessing Sun Filtered Memories That Tease,
Whisking Briskly Through The Cool Pine Trees
With Sighing Winds That Wheeze
While Bending My Boughs Today
Tenderly Blowing All Woes Away,
Through Fragrant Evergreen Forests Of Pines
Gently Whispering Your Name In Changing Times
Bestowing A Treasured Keepsake Key
Enabling Weary Eyes To Clearly See
The Beauty Of These Tumultuous God-Winds
Wondering How It Is That Spirit Sends
Treasured Thoughts Of You To Me
Silently Setting My Soul Free.

Mary Bee Johnson 4/23/06

BETTER DAYS

Years Go By Quickly Molding Themselves Into Memory
Pictures Filled With Good Times Shared Simply
Revealing Joys Blossoming Freely From Passing Days
In Our Brief Journey Through Life Always
Uniting The Good Times And Hard Times Above
Into A Beautiful Tapestry Of Days Woven with Love
By The Master Weaver's Skillful Hand
Supporting The Weary With Strength To Stand
When The Dark Threads Are As Necessary
As The Light Threads In Perfect Patterns Revelatory
Of A Life Lived In Faith Firmly Wed
With Hope Believing That Better Days Lie Ahead,
Where The Burdens Of Today Lie Fallow
As Trials Transform Into Blessings For Tomorrow!

Mary Bee Johnson 6/21/06

SISTERS

Stained glass memories frame sisters in time
Transcending all the days and manifold ways
Of Sisterhood wedded by years of joy
And sighs of Sorrow yet unity remains
Like stained glass window panes perfectly set
In secure times etched in heart protected
Places of utter joy when God placed
Sisters together where nothing can separate
The bond that binds this Holy Chapel
Formed by family hands eternally joined
From birth through life beyond death.

Mary Bee Johnson 8/15/07

WEDDING SONG

For even if I should take the Wings of the Morning
And fly to the uttermost parts of the Sea
Even there I will find you soaring
My Companion and Soul Friend where you will be
Singing Eagle Songs above the troubled winds
Guiding me homeward above the searing sun with Faithfulness
Always protecting Sacred Space where Love never ends
Eternally joining songs of Hope with Graciousness
Where Gentleness embraces Peace over difficult terrain
Above the turmoil of the long journey home forgiving all wrongs
On this earthly plane where open skies sustain
Heaven-Bound flights of joy while Wedding Songs
Whisper your name as Hero of the Wind
My Husband and Faithful Friend.

Mary Bee Johnson 10/27/06

LOVE

*Love is not what I was told in those days of old where romantic
Fantasies flitted thru a schoolgirl head of soft eternal hand
Holding sheltered in a sweet embrace on the hill where time
Stood still as rhapsodies would surround our union while
Serenades proclaim showering roses forever falling all around
But it was not so at all what they said when we were wed;
Rather a different tale unfurled of love hurled at tough times
War-tested In tumultuous jungles of Vietnam where duty called
Far too long as we grew strong apart with children joining our
Heart over the years while hardship cemented the fragile bonds
Of young love with the rash realities of too little money and too
Many bills yet the truth remains that love lived thru it all as we
Committed to join hearts "for better or worse till death do us
Part" and so today we still stand tall surveying it all, surprised
That the best days are just ahead while I hold your arm and
Whisper a silent thank you for standing by me thru it all in
Times of sickness, birth, and death where the coals of love's
Embers grew stronger still as God joined our hearts into an
Eternal diamond of love that shines brighter thru the furnace of
Many years glowing now as priceless eternal rings formed in
Fire yielding True Love tested by time and found to be forever.*

Mary Bee Johnson 8/24/07

PREPARATION

Crickets hum in the fresh evening
Stillness warm with late August
Wanderings of Monarch Butterflies
Flying free from green fields of
Milk Thistle nurseries while tiny hovering
Hummingbirds drink deeply at red
Bird feeders preparing for the
Courageous journey South as
Cardinals cheep and chipmunks
Chatter around the back porch
While fluffy chickadees filled with
Purpose splash in cleansing water
Fountains as squirrels rush to hide
Their acorns knowing the first hint
Of Autumn tinges the evening New England
Air as the Wise see and understand the
Need to prepare for a long Winter
Coming in our troubled Country.
Mary Bee Johnson 8/15/07

AMERICAN HEROES

*From the western highways and eastern by-ways of
Maine, New Hampshire, California, Colorado,
Kansas, Vermont, Nebraska, and Oklahoma in
This enormous land they came patriotically to serve
From Alabama, Mississippi, Georgia, and Ohio
Through all times and seasons of strife no matter
The Price they stood their ground defending
American ideals of human equality and freedom
Despite unfair treatment or mistaken goals
The Miracle remains they served with courage
From every race, state, and corner of our country
In tumultuous times facing uncertainty ahead
And dissension all around even as we proudly know
American soldiers still continue to stand with honor
Bravely in hostile lands defending a way of
Life that most do not understand protecting
Our right to dissent the course our nation walks
Even as the ranks of our Heroes today become
Filled with the old and weary supported by
The young and innocent from the West,
East, South, and North still willing to fight
Sacrificing life and limbs and future plans
To serve ideals of Honor and Freedom while
Too many politicians make deals to trade away our
Bill Of Rights for wiretapped phones and silence.*
Mary Bee Johnson 8/16/07

WISDOM CALLS
Wisdom cries out in the streets of America seeking
Agents of change Beneath broken city lights
Where homeless veterans sleep down under decaying bridges
Beneath cold snow filled by-ways where the forgotten citizen
Huddles under old newspapers to keep warm while
Corporate lobbyists provide dinner and provender
For senators who work for Pharmaceutical proliferation
As wealth becomes the privilege of a few with poverty
The right of the many; as Wisdom calls out
In gray granite Roads filthy with plastic waste
Of petroleum products imported by the rich profiting on cold
Shivering miseries of Americans buried in Winter Seasons
Beneath the glare of media cameras seeking quick answers
With popular sound bites as Wisdom weeps in alleys of America
Seeking true agents of change who will have the courage to walk
The highways with truth and integrity bringing lasting reform
To crumbling corrupted governmental bureaucracies drowning
In the blood of the Uninsured and Excluded while the rich dine
With a selected few who can pay the price of lobbying influence
As Wisdom cries out in the towns of America asking,
"Whom shall I send and who will go for me?"
Until the Chosen can reply, "Here am I, send me!
Send me to the poor and brokenhearted. Send me
To the weak and lame and forgotten.
Send me to the abandoned and Homeless,"
Until we can All stand together at last
With true Liberty and Justice for all."
Mary Bee Johnson 1/6/07

WHISPERS OF HOPE

Hope hangs like precious jewels in sparkling dawn
Dewdrops of morning rain cradled in morning glory
Petals preparing to open their hearts to another day
Turning delicate faces to the sun while climbing
Higher reaching always to the Heavens knowing their
Destiny is not long on this earth while courageously
Flowers shine and climb while transporting human
Thoughts higher than before as we watch in utter
Amazement the abundance they share faithfully
Turning fluttering faces to the glory of God's sunshine
Radiant with beauty freely offered as hummingbirds
Feed and nectars of life are generously given at this
Flowering fount of blessing where morning glories
Climb always in memories frozen in winter seasons
As whispering thoughts of flowered perfume bring
Hope that Spring does follow the Winters in our Life.

Mary Bee Johnson 1/22/08

THE PATH NOT TAKEN

Glowing fall colors invited us to go down the
Path so welcoming with harvest riches
Open to blue skies of amazing perfection
Reflecting Divine glorious gifts of another
Day of autumn beauty on our busy way, but time
Restrictions proved demanding with bills
Not paid, things undone, rooms uncleaned;
So we rushed past the by-way heading
Straight for the highway hurrying home to
Hear the same daily news of economies
Dissolving with war winds blowing closer
Exhausting Hope while the laundry washes
That will soon be dirty again whirling till night
Finally falls as sleep escapes a worried head
Awake on the pillow meandering with
Thoughts of blessings forever missed
Today on God's beautiful path not taken.

Mary Bee Johnson 8/22/07

WISHES

I wish you could walk the roads with me
Through the winding old neighborhood
Present once again, my friend, simply to see
The magic moments of this autumn day
Sharing the golden glimmering beauty
Fleeting though it may certainly be
Knowing that one shared moment is
Worth more than all the empty wishes
That ever could be for your presence
With me outside Time tries to transcend
The pain of separation when memories
Appear of the endless talks and walks
We shared living now again in the eternal
Fairy bound breezes blowing free
As I feel the touch of your absent hand
On a lonely October New Hampshire day.

Mary Bee Johnson 10/22/07

RECOVERY

*Small signs appear after the Time of Weeping
As awareness dawns briefly of the beauty of a
Summer day even though you are gone from
The place where you once sat beside me still I see
Gradually that the grass remains green and the
Morning Glories still bloom whispering your name
Even though life will never be quite the same yet
Somehow Morning comes with promises of new
Beginnings in the dewdrops of dawn glistening on
Expanses of emerald lawn you mowed only last
Year as I see and think of back porch cookouts
Where we laughed so hard we cried a tear or two
Sharing joy that still remains for it is true what the
Good Book says, "Weeping endures for a season but
Joy cometh in the Morning" when Comfort cradles
Grief like a child in the living heart of a caring God.*

Mary Bee Johnson 8/27/07

REMEMBERING DAYS

A rainy Remembering Day pours down deeds
Deeply drenched with memories of seeds
Of Morning Glory Love you planted long ago
Patiently waiting for the right moments so
Seeds can grow into a Sacred Garden on loan
In my mind with memories of a caring phone
Call and food shared with acts of comforting
In sad times when roaring rain came pouring
Through the open hole of my Soul where
Your hand held my heart with a note of fresh air
Breathing consolation carrying an open door
Flower filled to cheer away pain one day for
Evermore with seeds that bloom now leaving
Healing doors in my mind of eternally giving
Gifts growing at windows of my heart where soar
Morning Glories of Shared Love forevermore.

Mary Bee Johnson 7/23/07

HARVEST HELLOS

Beautiful eternal Autumn days
Misty with Mansions of Memories
Of family ties and so many familiar ways
Hover like sweet guitar harmonies
Singing West Virginia Appalachian tunes
Blues bound in warm October skies
Where huge round circular harvest moons
Rise on "All Saint's Day" with soft seductive sighs
Over the steeple of the white country church portraying
Family faces in autumn skies bridging divides from other sides
Of this limited Life with old by-ways where red leaves are falling
Like drifting memories of gold that gladly abides
In Heaven's abundant Clouds of Witnesses as it ranges
In distant corners of the free skies of Americana that welcomed
Dear ones gloriously Home in due season to dwell with Angels
As divine banners engraved with so many names stay unfurled
In sacred white drifting cotton candy clouds of Fall
Saluting you all, as familiar voices whisper in fresh free breezes
Bringing pictures of each of your smiles reflected in all
The shared joys Harvest Season memories releases.
Mary Bee Johnson 10/16/07

PROLOGUE

AMERICANA

Beyond the strip malls and suburban
Sprawl hiding behind smoggy cities and
Ever growing corporate giants buying
The sacred land all around us intent on ever
Growing profits while state governments
Scamper as the American Way struggles
To survive expanding political control;
The real Americana still lives in beautiful
By-Ways and winding hidden highways
Through pine filled trails verdant with old
Growth forests leading to fragrant fields
Of wildflower decked pristine prairies where
Patriots still live the dreams entrusted to
Our hearts by Pilgrim ancestors intent on
Establishing a Kingdom of God on earth,
As prophets are crying out today to this lost
Generation to "Stand by the Crossroads
And look, seek the ancient paths and
There you will find rest for your souls!"
Mary Bee Johnson

Made in the USA